*D*aughter...
I love you more than you know,
and I want everything beautiful
and wonderful for you,
today and always.

Mary Klock Labdon

Other books in the *"Language of"* Series...

Blue Mountain Arts®

It's Great to Have a Brother Like You

It's Great to Have a Sister like You

The Language of a Mother's Love

The Language of Brides

The Language of Courage and Inner Strength

The Language of Dance

The Language of Friendship

The Language of Happiness

The Language of Love

The Language of Marriage

The Language of Parenting

The Language of Positive Thinking

The Language of Prayer

The Language of Recovery

The Language of Success

The Language of Teaching

The Language of Teenagers

Thoughts to Share with a Wonderful Daughter

Thoughts to Share with a Wonderful Father

Thoughts to Share with a Wonderful Friend

Thoughts to Share with a Wonderful Mother

Thoughts to Share with a Wonderful Son

Words of Comfort ...For You in Your Time of Loss

You Will Always Have an Angel Watching Over You

The "Language of" Series...

Love and Wishes
For You,
Daughter

A Blue Mountain Arts® Collection
Inspired by the Joy and Hope a Daughter Brings to Life

Edited by Patricia Wayant

Blue Mountain Press™

SPS Studios, Inc., Boulder, Colorado

Library of Congress Control Number: 2002093187
ISBN: 0-88396-689-1

ACKNOWLEDGMENTS appear on page 48.

Certain trademarks are used under license.

Manufactured in Thailand.
First Printing: 2003

 This book is printed on recycled paper.

SPS Studios, Inc.

P.O. Box 4549, Boulder, Colorado 80306

❋ Contents ❋

(Authors listed in order of first appearance)

Wishing You, Daughter, a Life Filled with Laughter and Love

There are really no words that can express the love and wishes I hold for you.

We have gone through so much together, you and I — some times were laced with pain and sadness, but most were filled with the pure joy of our love for each other.

I remember how before you were born, I hoped for a daughter. Little did I know then that what I was really hoping for was a friend — someone to laugh with even when life was not funny, someone whose very presence would fill me with a love so deep and pure that I could finally understand what it meant to actually love someone more than I loved myself.

Because of your presence, the world is simply a better place. Because of the love and care you show to others, lives are touched and changed. Because of the generosity of your spirit, others feel hope.

When I hoped for a daughter, I never imagined that I would get so much more. May you always know that I love you and I am so very proud of you, my daughter and my friend.

 Lea Walsh

Daughter, These Special Wishes
Are Just for You

When you close your eyes at the
   end of each day, I wish you
   contented and peaceful sleep.
When you are fearful or uncertain,
   I wish for warmth and light
   to surround you.
When you dream, I wish you
   soaring images and endless possibilities.
When you wake each morning,
   I wish you the joy of anticipating
   a beautiful day ahead.
When you face problems, I wish you
   boundless strength and courage
   to guide you.
When you walk along your path,
   I wish you lasting friendships
   to brighten your way.
Most of all, I wish you love...
   to fill your heart
   and make your world complete.

— Linda Sackett-Morrison

May All Your Dreams
Be Beautiful

May your days be filled with good health
and strength to meet the challenges that
may come your way...
With safety, friendship, and light to guide you
in the right direction...
With unexpected pleasures and the grace and
humility to see the beauty in all things —
whether they are simple or grand...
With self-confidence and self-knowledge to lift
your spirit and lighten your steps, as you
move forward and reach for your dreams...
With understanding and courage to see you
through the rough times...
With family and love to carry and keep within
your heart... each and every day.

 Linda Sackett-Morrison

There's Something Special About a Daughter

You know I love all my
children. But there is
something very special
about [my daughter].
It's as though all the
good fairies were standing
around her cradle when
she was born and they
just gave her everything.
She is a life enhancer.
She is a window into
another world.

♡ Naomi Ruth Lowinsky, Ph.D.

A Daughter's Gift

When I imagine
the life you will live,
I think of the pleasure
your presence will give;
I see the joy
your smile will light
and the wonders you'll weave
when your dreams take flight.
I feel the hope
that will grow with your grace
and the difference you'll make
to each heart you embrace.
I imagine your life
as I know it will be;
for, my daughter, you've given
all this to me.

♡ Robert Sexton

A daughter is a little piece
    of yourself
looking back at you.
She is another chance for you
        to realize the dreams
            of your past.
She is God's most precious gift,
    and adventures without end.

A daughter is your best creation.
She's a best friend
    and a fashion advisor.

Only she knows why
    you love purple
        and hate turnips.

A daughter is never-ending love,
    given and received,
and learning to love yourself.
Of all the things that
    happen in life,
        a daughter is the best.

 Brenda A. Morris

Daughter,
Your Happiness Is What
I Wish for Most

I wish for you to always see
   the goodness in this world,
to do your part in helping those
   less fortunate,
to walk hand in hand with those
   of less talent,
to follow those with more knowledge,
   and to be an equal with those
who are different.

I wish for you to find your special purpose
   in this world so full of choices
and to help lead those who stray.
I wish for you to become your
   own individual —
to set yourself apart from those who
   are the same.

I wish for you the self-confidence to say "no"
   when it is necessary, and the strength
      to stand alone.
I wish for you the approval of yourself
   to love and respect everything that
      you are and will become.
I wish for you to reap the fruits of your talents,
to walk with pride down the road of life,
to be humble in your successes,
and to share in the praises and joy of others.
Most of all, I wish for you to be happy.
For when you are happy,
   you have the key that will open all
      of the world's doors to you.

 Jackie Olson

Did You Know that I Loved You Long Before You Were Born?

You were a part of my future
    when I was just a little girl.
When I first held you in my arms,
one of my childhood dreams came true.
I remember staring at your
    perfect little features
and feeling thrilled at each new sound
    and expression.
A fierce need to protect you
    came over me then,
and it has never gone away.
When you were a child,
I was able to hold you close
    through illness and heartache.
I could hold your hand as you faced new experiences,
and my presence and guidance seemed to
assure you of a certain level of safety.

But little by little, I have had to let you go
and allow you to make your own way.
So often I wanted to call you back and have you stay
in the protective circle of my arms.
I never wanted you to have to face injury or heartache,
yet I knew that you had to in order to grow.
Now you are all grown up
and making your own decisions, often facing life alone.
Just remember that no matter what, I love you.
I could never stop loving you.
You are the hugs and smiles from my past,
    the hopes and dreams of my future.
Take care, my daughter,
and know that you are never alone.
We are connected together by the strongest bond there is:
the love between a parent and child.

— Barbara Cage

Always Believe in Yourself and Your Dreams, Daughter...

As you go on in this world, keep looking forward to the future... to all you might be. Don't let old mistakes or misfortunes hold you down: learn from them, forgive yourself — or others — and move on. Do not be bothered or discouraged by adversity. Instead, meet it as a challenge. Be empowered by the courage it takes you to overcome obstacles. Learn things. Learn something new every day.

Be interested in others and what they might teach you. But do not look for yourself in the faces of others. Do not look for who you are in other people's approval. As far as who you are and who you will become goes — the answer is always within yourself. Believe in yourself. Follow your heart and your dreams. You — like everyone else — will make mistakes. But as long as you are true to the strength within your own heart... you can never go wrong.

Ashley Rice

...and Know that You Are Loved

Know yourself —
what you can do
and want to do in life
Set goals
and work hard to achieve them
Have fun every day in every way
Be creative —
it is an expression
   of your feelings
Be sensitive in viewing the world
Believe in the family
as a stable and rewarding way
of life
Believe in love
as the most complete
and important emotion possible
Believe that you are
an important part of
everyone's life that you touch
Believe in yourself
and know that you are loved

Susan Polis Schutz

Loving Memories of a Daughter like You

When I taught you
at eight to ride
a bicycle, loping along
beside you
as you wobbled away
on two round wheels,
my own mouth rounding
in surprise when you pulled
ahead down the curved
path of the park,
I kept waiting
for the thud
of your crash as I
sprinted to catch up,
while you grew
smaller, more breakable
with distance,
pumping, pumping
for your life, screaming
with laughter,
the hair flapping
behind you like a
handkerchief waving
goodbye.

— Linda Pastan

Breathing

I left your door open tonight.
I wanted to hear the breathing, like the first days,
the baby days, when your breath was everything
and I listened in the deep
night hours at the foot
of your small nest of quilts
until all danger passed over
your new body. Then I could sleep.
Tonight I move restless through the hours.
Words you sing between tosses and turns
send electricity through me, a shudder.

Back then I measured your heartbeat
with my own, watched your chest rise
and fall as it took hold, took root
in the pull of the moon and tides.
I brought colors to your crib,
news of the outside world, the first taste
of apricots, the Northcoast gales.
I imagined you flew at night
with all the other babies
wrapped in white linen kimonos
above the wet rooftops of our dreary mill town.
And I would wait, ready to talk
us through this passage of dream.

Stephen J. Lyons

What do I dream for my daughter and her future?

Obviously I want the very best for her. I want her to be what SHE wants to be, to realize HER dreams, and if I can be there to help her, guide and support her, perhaps I will be fulfilling one of my dreams. I want for her to have the opportunities I never had, to learn from my mistakes. I want her to find true friendship and true love.

I want for her to see [the world's] beauty and appreciate the endless number of wonderful creatures and places that it holds. I want for her to care for it, fight for it and protect it so that her children and grandchildren will also know its wonders. I wish her a world of peace, where Man has learned to live in harmony with the Earth and all that coexist here, whether it be plant, creature or fellow Man. I want her to remember my teachings in that true happiness is not found in material wealth but in the beauty of the flower, bird song, dew on a spider's web, dolphins playing — the richness of nature — for this is what would be missed the most if it were not there.

Christine P. Dodwell

Remember, Daughter...

It's not how much you accomplish in life
that really counts,
but how much you give to others.
It's not how high you build your dreams
that makes a difference,
but how high your faith can climb.
It's not how many goals you reach,
but how many lives you touch.
It's not who you know that matters,
but who you are inside.

 — Rebecca Barlow Jordan

The finest things in life are those
You neither sell nor buy,
A bursting bud — a bird that sings,
A glowing Western sky;
And friends to love, these are, indeed,
Well worth their weight in gold,
And may you know the joys which
You will forever behold.

 — Caroline Bowes Tombo

I Hope You Make Your Mark on the World

It is my hope that you discover
    your talents
and have the courage and confidence
to pursue your every dream.
You have the power
to create your own destiny.
You are strong.
You are loving.
You are kind.
You sprinkle hope for the future
    everywhere you go.
You are my single greatest
    accomplishment,
and the sun shines a little brighter
    each time I think of you.

♡ Kim Peek

If you have anything really
valuable to contribute to the
world, it will come through
the expression of your own
personality — that single
spark of divinity that sets
you off and makes you
different from every other
living creature.

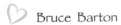 Bruce Barton

You have so much to offer,
so much to give, and
so much you deserve
to receive in return.
Don't ever doubt that.

Know yourself and all your fine
    qualities.
Rejoice in all your marvelous strengths
    of mind and body.
Be glad for the virtues that are yours,
    and pat yourself on the back for all
    your many admirable achievements.

Keep positive.
Concentrate on that which
    makes you happy,
        and build yourself up.
Stay nimble of heart,
    happy of thought,
    healthy of mind, and
        well in being.

 Janet A. Sullivan

Love and Wishes
for You, Daughter...

As a parent, there are so many dreams
that I want to come true for you.
I want you to be independent and self-assured.
I want you to live life to the fullest.
And, as time goes by
and you don't need my guidance
and direction as much as before,
I hope you will always remember...
I love you.

Deanna Beisser

I wish you success and happiness
wherever you go, whatever you do.

M. Joye

May you always know
how appreciated you are.
May love walk by your side.
May friendship sing in your smile.
May opportunity remember to knock on your
door and surprise you once in a while.

Collin McCarty

My wish for you is a simple one:
   I wish that you will be
   the person you were meant to be.
Everything else will follow;
   your dreams will come true.

   — Karen Poynter Taylor

I know your days are busy, but I hope that they are giving back to you
as much as you give to them. And I know that there are moments when
things could be better, but I hope you'll remember that good things come
to good people, and that — without a doubt — you are one of the best.

   — Laurel Atherton

I wish you all the love
and fulfillment
that having you as a daughter
has brought to me.

   — Katherine J. Romboldi

I Hope Nothing Ever Changes Your Inner Beauty

You are such an outstanding person
and I hope nothing ever changes
your inner beauty
As you keep growing
remember always
to look at things the way you do now —
with sensitivity
honesty
compassion
and a touch of innocence
Remember that people and situations
may not always be
as they appear
but if you remain true to yourself
it will be all right

With your outlook, you will see
the good in everything
and this will reflect back to you
When I look ahead
I see happiness for you on every level
and I am so glad
because that is what every mother
wishes for her daughter
I love you

 Susan Polis Schutz

Beauty is seen
In the sunlight,
The trees, the birds,
Corn growing and people working
Or dancing for their harvest.

Beauty is heard
In the night,
Wind sighing, rain falling,
Or a singer chanting
Anything in earnest.

Beauty is in yourself.
Good deeds, happy thoughts
That repeat themselves
In your dreams,
In your work,
And even in your rest.

 Louise Abeita

May You Find Joy in Every Moment...

May you follow tomorrow
wherever it takes you
and wake up every morning
to a day full of song.
May your life become
a field of miracles
stretching out with possibilities.
May you kick off your shoes
and open your heart
to feel the joy that comes
    from realizing
how very much you're loved.
May you discover many gifts
    on your doorstep
for all the ways you've been
    a gift to me.
A heart that is always caring
and a life that is always sharing —
    like yours —
deserves a happy day.
Enjoy!

Linda E. Knight

...and May You Always ♡♡ Have Your Own Star ♡♡ to Guide You

May all your tomorrows be filled
with more wonders than
    you've ever imagined.
May your life hold an infinite supply
    of unlimited dreams.
As you work so hard to achieve
    your goals,
may you celebrate yourself
and all that you do.
Once in a while,
look back over your shoulder
and congratulate yourself
on how far you've come.

Look to your talents and gifts
and honor them as treasures.
Be blessed always
in all the ways you have grown.
Wherever life takes you,
may you always have
your own star to guide you
each step of the way.

♡ Linda E. Knight

I Want You to Live a Life of Love, My Daughter

We brought you into this world
a beautiful little girl
born of love
who would one day
grow up to be
a beautiful woman full of love

I tried to teach you
important values and morals
I tried to show you
how to be strong and honest, gentle
    and sensitive
I tried to explain to you
the importance of achieving your
    own goals

I tried to express
the need to reach out to people
I tried to emphasize
the beauty of nature
I tried to demonstrate
the extreme importance of family
And I tried, every day, to set
    an example
that you could look up to

When we brought you into the world
I did not think about how everything
could be destroyed in a few minutes
in a world not at peace
in a world with nuclear weapons

I taught you love
in a sometimes hateful world
because it is love that can abolish hate
before hate abolishes us

I am very sorry, my beautiful daughter
that these destructive forces
have been handed down to you
All of the mothers
and all of the fathers
in the entire world
must unite together and
dedicate ourselves to
ending violence as a way
of solving problems
We must do this so that we can assure you
my daughter, and all children
that you will grow up
to hike in the mountains
and run in the fields of flowers
so that we can assure you
that you will have a chance to grow up
to live a life
of peace and
love

Susan Polis Schutz

May You Have Everything You Need to Lead a Full Life

Enough happiness to keep you sweet,
Enough trials to keep you strong,
Enough sorrow to keep you human,
Enough hope to keep you happy;
Enough failure to keep you humble,
Enough success to keep you eager,
Enough friends to give you comfort,
Enough wealth to meet your needs;
Enough enthusiasm to look forward,
Enough faith to banish depression,
Enough determination to make each day
    better than yesterday.

Author Unknown

The pleasantest things in the world are pleasant thoughts: and
the great art of life is to have as many of them as possible.

 Michel de Montaigne

Fatherly Advice

The final list of fatherly advice: clip coupons and always buy generic. Memorize some lines of poetry. Learn to play a musical instrument. Exercise, but never weigh yourself. Make a lot of money and then give it all away. Learn the names of flowers, plants, and birds. Sleep with the windows open. Recycle. Eat out only in small town cafes where the waitress is also the cook, bartender, and day care coordinator. Volunteer in the community. Cultivate solitude. Forgive yourself. Bring your own bag to the grocery store.... Don't run the water needlessly when brushing your teeth. Use less of everything. Hug a tree. Don't spit. Be of good cheer.

 Stephen J. Lyons

Let there be many windows to your soul,
That all the glory of the universe
May beautify it.

 Ella Wheeler Wilcox

Wish List

Of all the things I wish for you, I would give anything if these wishes could always come true...

I want you to be happy. I want you to fill your heart with feelings of wonder and to be full of courage and hope. I want you to have the type of friendship that is a treasure — and the kind of love that is beautiful forever. I wish you contentment: the sweet, quiet, inner kind that comes around and never goes away.

I want you to have hopes and have them all come true. I want you to make the most of every moment in time. I want you to have a real understanding of how unique and rare you truly are. I want to remind you that the sun may disappear for a while, but it never forgets to shine. I want you to have faith. May you have feelings that are shared from heart to heart, simple pleasures amidst this complex world, and wonderful goals that are within your grasp. May the words you listen to say the things you need to hear. And may a cheerful face lovingly look back at you when you happen to glance in your mirror.

I wish you the insight to see your inner and outer beauty. I wish you sweet dreams. I want you to have times when you feel like singing and dancing and laughing out loud. I want you to be able to make your good times better and your hard times easier to handle. I want you to have millions of moments when you find satisfaction in the things you do so wonderfully. And I wish I could find a way to tell you — in untold ways — how important you are to me.

Of all the things I'll be wishing for, wherever you are and whatever I may do, there will never be a day in my life when I won't be wishing for the best... for you.

♡ ♡ Collin McCarty

I Want the World to Know
What I Already Do...
How Absolutely Wonderful You Are

I think you're amazing and rare and beautiful. You
have a way of making every day feel like Christmas.
I think your spirit is inspiring, that your light shines
so bright, and that you're such a dream come true.

And I want you to know that I feel very lucky to
have been given the gift of having a daughter
like you.

R. L. Keith

You are the sparkle in my eyes
and the pride in my heart.
You are the courage
that gives me strength
and the love that gives me life.
You are my inspiration
and the best gift I ever received.

 Lois Carruthers

I often wish for those days again
when I could pick you up
over my head, hear you
laugh your baby laugh,
and see that halo of light
the sun brought to your hair.
I wish for those days when
I could swing you around and around,
laughing and screaming
as if there weren't a care in the world!
I wish I could bring to you
the innocence and the safety
that only babies know...

but with each fall you take and
each disappointment you suffer,
you learn that life is not so simple.
As long as you remember that
time will always pass, that
things can always change, and that
you can make a difference,
then you will have hope.
And with hope,
you can keep that beauty in yourself
and
the beauty in your smile,
and you will make a difference...
You already have.

Linda Pomeroy

20 Beautiful Things
That Are True About You

You are something — and someone — very special.
You really are. No one else in this entire world is
exactly like you, and there are so many beautiful
things about you.

You're a one-of-a-kind treasure, uniquely here in
this space and time. You are here to shine in your
own wonderful way, sharing your smile in the best
way you can, and remembering all the while that
a little light somewhere makes a brighter light
everywhere. You can — and you do — make
a wonderful contribution to this world.

You have qualities within you that many people
would love to have, and those who really and truly
know you... are so glad that they do. You have a
big heart and a good and sensitive soul. You are
gifted with thoughts and ways of seeing things that
only special people know. You know that life doesn't
always play by the rules, but that in the long run,
everything will work out.

You understand that you and your actions are capable of turning anything around — and that joys once lost can always be found. There is a resolve and an inner reserve of strength in you that few ever get to see. You have so many treasures within — those you're only beginning to discover, and all the ones you're already aware of.

Never forget what a treasure you are. That special person in the mirror may not always get to hear all the compliments you so sweetly deserve, but

you are so worthy of
such an abundance
...of friendship, joy, and love.

Douglas Pagels

My Dreams for My Daughters, Granddaughters, and All Women

1) That you can maintain your independence and develop a solid feeling of self-worth.

2) Find satisfaction and contentment in your personal lives and in whatever career or careers you pursue.

3) Have a life that is rich and rewarding, filled with love of family and friends, combined with compassion and tolerance for others.

4) That you never cease to learn, maintain a wide range of interests, and remain open to new experiences and risks.

5) That you develop and maintain a good set of values in making judgements and resist compromise that is inconsistent with your values.

6) Identify the priorities that guide your actions and update them throughout life.

7) Have the strength and judgement to cope objectively with problems as they occur.

8) Always maintain a sense of humor, remembering that we pass through this life only once and that life is transitional.

9) Remember that you are in charge of your own attitude; the only person you can control is yourself.

10) Be a part of the changing "community" with an awareness of what is good, what needs changing, and what you can contribute to make it better. Be involved.

11) Count your blessings and remember those who helped you acquire them and the need to pass that help along.

Ina May Rouse

Wherever You Go, Daughter, You'll Never Be Far from My Heart

With a smile, I remember the day you were born... crying softly as I held you for the first time, peering into your soft, little eyes with love.

Each minute of your life is etched in my memory — from the very first smile to the day you left home to test your own wings, smiling as you waved and said, "I love you," the light of your love shining through your smile.

It wasn't easy, letting you go off on your own, though I realized that you were grown and ready to see the world. And even though I wanted to run after you and say, "Stop! I'm not ready for this yet," I didn't, because I love you.

You are my shining light, my child. You are what I always dreamed you would be... strong of spirit, full of love, seeking knowledge of a world that is changing around you every second.

I'm glad I've got you in my life. Loving you, watching you grow, even arguing with you have all made my life so beautiful. I love you my child... always and ever.

Michele Richards Shapiro

You'll always be love
cradled in my heart
and memories to cherish
   through the years.
You'll always be a sunbeam,
smiles for the soul,
and hugs reaching up
   to outstretched arms.
You'll always be the cord
that binds and ties the years.
You'll always be dreams
gently growing into flowers
in a garden of special secrets
   to share.

You'll always be footsteps
racing through time
beneath the moon of yesterday.
You'll always be kisses
blowing in the wind
on a playground stretched out
   from sky to sky.
You'll always be the gift
God has given me
and years growing onward,
   full and deep.
You'll always be my joy,
my happiness, my song.
You'll always be the child I love.

 Linda E. Knight

I Believe in You, Daughter

As you make your way to the places where dreams come true, don't be afraid to make mistakes. They are lessons that teach you how to do better. If you seize these opportunities to learn about life, mistakes will lead you to new and exciting places where you'll find beautiful things.

Don't look for approval from everyone you meet. Not everyone will love you, but they can teach you something about getting along with others. If you observe people, listen to them, and learn to understand their needs, you will always come out ahead. You may even make some unexpected friends.

You must always love yourself. Give your mind good thoughts; give your body good nourishment and exercise. Give your spirits good poetry, music, and healthy doses of laughter. Give your soul the serenity and healing of prayer.

Make your way through life with patience, kindness, and friendly smiles. Enjoy the scenery along the way. Give thanks for the blessings of each new day. Let faith, hope, quiet strength, and a peaceful soul be your pilots as you travel each winding path. Hold on to the happy memories of the past, the sweet expectations you have of the future, and the happiness of today.

On your journey to the places of your deepest dreams, may you always hear me calling your name and saying, "I believe in you." May you always feel the warmth of my embrace and the reassurance of my never-ending love for you.

Jacqueline Schiff

May Angels Guide and Keep You...

May angels guide and keep you.
May they walk beside you in light
   and in darkness,
and may they bring healing peace
to all your cares and every anxious fear.
May they whisper words of hope,
   assurance, and love.
May they inspire your heart and mind
   with new ideas,
and lead you along paths of blessing
   and abundance.
May angels walk beside you
   and bring you joy
in the desert, on the sea,
on the mountaintop and in the valley,
through the forest and along the shore.
May angels guide and keep you,
and may they walk beside you
all the days and nights of your life.

Deborah A. Bennett

...and May You Always Know
How Much I Love You

I love you more than you know,
and I want everything beautiful
and wonderful for you,
today and always.
I love being in your life and
sharing all that comes your way.
The love I have for you is so great
that I never have, and I never will,
take for granted the blessing
you have been to me.
I hope that as the years go by,
we will become even closer.
I couldn't have picked
a more precious daughter.
Thank you for giving me this chance
to say, "I love you,
and I will always be here for you."

Mary Klock Labdon

ACKNOWLEDGMENTS

We gratefully acknowledge the permission granted by the following authors, publishers, and authors' representatives to reprint poems or excerpts from their publications.

Linda Sackett-Morrison for "May All Your Days Be Beautiful." Copyright © 2002 by Linda Sackett-Morrison. All rights reserved.

Felichia Eth Literaray Agency for "You know I love all my children…" from THE MOTHERLINE by Naomi Ruth Lowinsky, Ph.D., published by Jeremy P. Tarcher, a division of Penguin Putnam, Inc. Copyright © 1992 by Naomi Ruth Lowinsky. All rights reserved.

Robert Sexton for "A Daughter's Gift." Copyright © 1995 by Robert Sexton. All rights reserved.

Brenda A. Morris for "A daughter is a little piece of yourself…." Copyright © 2002 by Brenda A. Morris. All rights reserved.

W. W. Norton & Company for "When I taught you…" from THE IMPERFECT PARADISE by Linda Pastan. Copyright © 1988 by Linda Pastan. All rights reserved.

Washington University Press for "Breathing" and "Fatherly Advice" from LANDSCAPE OF THE HEART by Stephen J. Lyons. Copyright © 1996 by the Board of Regents of Washington State University. All rights reserved.

Bonnie Coffey for "What do I dream for my daughter…" by Christine P. Dodwell and "My Dreams for My Daughter, Granddaughters, and All Women" by Ina May Rouse from DREAMS FOR OUR DAUGHTERS, edited by Bonnie Coffey. Copyright © 2001 by Bonnie A. Coffey. All rights reserved.

Kim Peek for "It is my hope that you discover your talents…." Copyright © 2002 by Kim Peek. All rights reserved.

William Morrow & Co., Inc., for "Beauty is seen…" from I AM A PUEBLO INDIAN GIRL by Louise Abeita. Copyright © 1939 by William Morrow & Co., Inc. Renewed 1967 by Louise Abeita Chiwiwi. All rights reserved.

Linda E. Knight for "May You Find Joy in Every Moment…" and "…and May You Always Have Your Own Star to Guide You." Copyright © 2002 by Linda E. Knight. All rights reserved.

Linda Pomeroy for "I often wish for those days again…." Copyright © 2002 by Linda Pomeroy. All rights reserved.

Michele Richards Shapiro for "With a smile, I remember the day you were born…." Copyright © 2002 by Michele Richards Shapiro. All rights reserved.

Jacqueline Schiff for "Some Final Thoughts Just for You, Daughter." Copyright © 2002 by Jacqueline Schiff. All rights reserved.

Deborah A. Bennett for "May Angels Guide and Keep You…." Copyright © 2002 by Deborah A. Bennett. All rights reserved.

A careful effort has been made to trace the ownership of selections used in this anthology in order to obtain permission to reprint copyrighted materials and give proper credit to the copyright owners. If any error or omission has occurred, it is completely inadvertent, and we would like to make corrections in future editions provided that written notification is made to the publisher:

SPS STUDIOS, INC., P.O. Box 4549, Boulder, Colorado 80306.